EXPLORING WORLD CULTURES

Taiwan

By Joanne Mattern

Cavendish Square

New York

Published in 2022 by Cavendish Square Publishing, LLC
243 5th Avenue, Suite 136, New York, NY 10016

Library of Congress Cataloging-in-Publication Data

Names: Mattern, Joanne, 1963- author.
Title: Taiwan / Joanne Mattern.
Description: First Edition. | New York : Cavendish Square Publishing, 2022.
| Series: Exploring world cultures | Includes index.
Identifiers: LCCN 2020038487 | ISBN 9781502659040 (Library Binding) | ISBN
9781502659026 (Paperback) | ISBN 9781502659033 (Set) | ISBN
9781502659057 (eBook)
Subjects: LCSH: Taiwan--Juvenile literature. | Taiwan--Description and
travel. | Taiwan--History--Juvenile literature. | Taiwan--Social life
and customs.
Classification: LCC DS799 .M38 2022 | DDC 951.249--dc23
LC record available at https://lccn.loc.gov/2020038487

Editor: Katie Kawa
Copy Editor: Nicole Horning
Designer: Jessica Nevins

The photographs in this book are used by permission and through the courtesy of: Cover imtmphoto/Shutterstock.com;
p. 4 PATRICK LIN/AFP via Getty Images; pp. 5, 9 GoranQ/E+/Getty Images; p. 6 kosmozoo/DigitalVision Vectors/Getty
Images; pp. 7, 16 Alberto Buzzola/LightRocket via Getty Images; p. 8 Stockbyte/Getty Images; p. 10 ak_phuong/Moment/
Getty Images; p. 11 Patrick Aventurier/Getty Images; p. 12 Feature China/Barcroft Media via Getty Images; p. 13 Universal
Education/Universal Images Group via Getty Images; p. 14 wrangel/iStock/Getty Images Plus/Getty Images; p. 15 Charlie
Jung/500px/Getty Images; p. 17 fotoVoyager/E+/Getty Images; p. 18 JohnnyGreig/E+/Getty Images; p. 19 Portra/E+/Getty
Images; p. 20 Mlenny/E+/Getty Images; p. 21 Prisma by Dukas/Universal Images Group via Getty Images; p. 22 golero/E+/
Getty Images; p. 23 Yongyuan Dai/Moment Editorial/Getty Images; p. 24 SAM YEH/AFP via Getty Images; p. 25 Chang Hsiu
Huang/Moment Editorial/Getty Images; p. 26 CHARLY TRIBALLEAU/AFP via Getty Images; p. 27 Ippei Naoi/Moment/Getty
Images; p. 28 totororo/Moment/Getty Images; p. 29 d3sign/Moment/Getty Images.

CPSIA compliance information: Batch #CS22CSQ: For further information contact Cavendish Square Publishing LLC,
New York, New York, at 1-877-980-4450.

Printed in the United States of America

Find us on

Contents

Taiwan is an island located off the coast of mainland China in Asia. Its history can be hard to understand. At one time, Taiwan was united with the rest of China. Then, a civil war—a war between two groups in the same

Is Taiwan its own country? Although the PRC says no, many Taiwanese people believe they have their own national identity, or sense of self.

country—broke out. The losing side, known as the Republic of China (ROC), moved to Taiwan.

Some countries around the world view the ROC as its own nation separate from the People's Republic of China (PRC), which is based on the mainland. However, the PRC doesn't share this view and claims Taiwan as part of its country.

Shown here is Taipei, which is Taiwan's capital. It's easy to spot Taipei 101, which was the tallest building in the world until 2010.

Taiwan is a very unique, or special, place. It has many mountains, forests, and bodies of water. Many animals live there. It's home to both modern cities and **traditional** ways of life.

People in Taiwan enjoy tasty foods. They spend time with their family and friends. They play sports and games. Let's learn more about Taiwan and its people!

The ROC is commonly called Taiwan, but it's bigger than just one island. It covers 13,976 square miles (36,197 square kilometers), including the island of Taiwan and other islands governed by the ROC.

This map of Taiwan shows how the island is broken into different areas for governing. It also shows the waterways surrounding the island, such as the Luzon Strait, which includes the Bashi Channel.

The island of Taiwan is bordered by the Pacific Ocean and Philippine Sea to the east. The East

FACT!

Yu Shan (or Yushan) is the tallest mountain in Taiwan. It's 12,966 feet (3,952 meters) high.

China Sea lies to the north. The Bashi Channel is a waterway that separates southern Taiwan from the Philippines. The Taiwan Strait (or Formosa Strait) in

Yu Shan is also called Jade Mountain.

the west lies between Taiwan and China.

The Chung-yang Range (or Central Range) is a group of mountains that run down the eastern part of the island. The western part has rolling hills and areas of flat land.

Shake It Up

Taiwan generally has more than 15,000 earthquakes each year. Most of these movements of the earth are too small to be felt, but some bigger earthquakes in Taiwan have been deadly.

Historians believe people have lived on the island of Taiwan for about 30,000 years. However, we don't know much about the earliest settlers.

Shown here is the Taiwanese flag.

Chinese people traveled to Taiwan as far back as 239 CE. Europeans came, too, and the Dutch eventually claimed Taiwan for themselves. At one time, Taiwan was also part of Japan. Finally, it became part of the ROC in 1945.

FACT!

Around 5,000 years ago, the Dapenkeng culture, or way of life, took root in Taiwan.

In 1949, a **Communist** government took over China. The leader of the ROC at that time, Chiang Kai-shek, fled to Taiwan. Around 2 million people followed him.

Chiang Kai-shek Memorial Hall is an important landmark in Taipei built to honor the former leader of the ROC.

The new government in China—the PRC—didn't recognize Taiwan's government. Even today, the PRC has said that other countries can't recognize both the PRC and the ROC.

9

VOTE ✓

The ROC's government was set up by a constitution, or a document that spells out how a country will be run. This constitution went into effect in 1947.

The Presidential Office Building is where the president of Taiwan works. As the head of state, the president serves as the face of Taiwan to the rest of the world.

The government has five branches, called Yuans. The executive branch includes the premier, who leads the government, and their advisers. Taiwan also has a president, who names the

FACT!

Taiwan offers civil service exams, which people must pass to get a government job.

premier and serves as the head of state. The president is elected by the people.

The legislative, or lawmaking, branch has 113 members. They're elected and serve four-year terms.

In 2019, the Taiwanese government made it legal for same-sex couples to get married. This was a big day for equality in Taiwan!

The judicial branch handles the courts. In addition, the constitution set up an Examination Yuan to run civil service exams and a Control Yuan to monitor, or watch, other parts of the government.

Taiwan's National Anthem

In 1924, Chinese leader Sun Yat-sen gave a speech filled with hope and national pride. That speech became the ROC's national anthem, or song.

Taiwan has a healthy economy, or system of making, buying, and selling goods. In fact, it's one of Asia's major economic powers.

Factories in Taiwan make parts for computers.

More than half of Taiwan's people work in service jobs. The service industry, or business, includes stores, restaurants, and hotels. It also includes banks, hospitals, and schools. Other people in Taiwan work in factories. They make **electronic** goods and machines.

FACT!

China and Taiwan have had their differences, but China is Taiwan's top trading partner.

Beautiful Money

Taiwan's currency, or money, is called the New Taiwan dollar. Paper bills come in different colors. They have pictures of important people and places.

Taiwan sells these products to people all over the world.

Farming is a small part of Taiwan's economy. Rice and tea are the most common crops. Farmers

Shown here are examples of the money used in Taiwan.

also grow fruits, such as watermelons, and vegetables, such as cabbages and green onions. Some farmers raise pigs, chickens, and ducks. Flowers, especially orchids, grown in Taiwan have also become popular goods to sell.

13

The Environment

Taiwan is home to many unique plants and animals. The largest mammal on the island is the Formosan black bear. It lives in the mountain forests. These forests are

The muntjac is a **protected** animal in Taiwan.

also home to a monkey called the macaque and a kind of deer called the muntjac.

Around 500 kinds of birds have been found on the island of Taiwan. These birds include magpies, pheasants, and ducks. Taiwan is also home

FACT!

Air pollution is a big problem in Taiwan. Sometimes you can see it hanging over cities!

Saving Coral Reefs

The coral reefs around Taiwan are in trouble because of human activity. The government is trying to save these important parts of nature and keep the water around them clean.

to many kinds of reptiles and amphibians. Snakes, frogs, and toads are found all over the island. Big bugs, such as giant stag beetles and colorful butterflies, are common too.

Taiwan's coral reefs, such as the one shown here, are in danger. However, the people of Taiwan are trying to keep this part of the environment, or natural world, around for a long time.

Many different plants grow on this island. Taiwan is filled with bamboo, palm trees, oaks, and pines. Taiwan has created national parks to protect its plants and animals.

More than 23 million people live in Taiwan. Almost all of them are **ethnically** Taiwanese and come from a Han Chinese background. The Han Chinese ethnic

Members of indigenous groups in Taiwan sometimes wear traditional clothing.

group is the world's largest ethnic group and can be traced back to the Chinese mainland.

Taiwan is also home to many indigenous, or native groups. These groups lived on the island

FACT!

The Indigenous Television Network is a TV channel in Taiwan that highlights indigenous cultures.

Most of the people living in Taiwan today live in one of its cities. For example, more than 4 million people live in New Taipei City!

of Taiwan before the Han Chinese people arrived. The Amis are the largest indigenous group.

About 800,000 foreigners, or people from other countries, live in

Taiwan's cities are busy places filled with many people.

Taiwan. Many come from other Asian countries. Others come from Europe and the United States. Many new immigrants, or people who come to live in Taiwan from somewhere else, come from mainland China.

17

Lifestyle

Taiwan is a crowded island. Many people live in its cities. They often live in apartments in big buildings. They shop in stores and open-air

Many women in Taiwan work outside of the home.

markets. City streets are filled with cars, bikes, and buses. At night, the cities glow with bright lights.

The family is a central part of life in Taiwan. Children are taught to respect and honor their parents and to take care of them as they get older.

FACT!

There are more than 100 colleges and universities in Taiwan for students to attend after high school.

Families have gotten smaller over time, with each family in Taiwan now only having an average of one child.

Students from Taiwan often do very well on tests, especially in science and math.

Education is very important in Taiwan. Children work hard in school and study for many hours. They do this to pass tests that will get them into good colleges.

Cram Schools

Many students in Taiwan attend another kind of school too. These schools are called cram schools. Students at these schools can take lessons in many subjects, such as English.

Religion

People in Taiwan follow different religions, or belief systems. Religious freedom is available to all in Taiwan. One of the most popular religions is Buddhism, which

Temples such as this one are found throughout Taiwan. Temples are holy places.

was founded in India more than 2,000 years ago. Buddhists believe people should work for peace. They should do kind deeds and care for others.

Taoism (also known as Daoism) is another popular religion in Taiwan. This religion began in

FACT!

People in Taiwan honor their ancestors, or family members who lived long before them.

Confucianism

Many people in Taiwan follow a philosophy, or way of life, called Confucianism. It was founded more than 2,000 years ago by a Chinese thinker called Confucius. It's not a religion, but it's founded on important values such as respect and family.

China. Taoism calls for a simple life and following the natural order of the world.

Many people in Taiwan also follow Chinese folk religions. These religions have many gods and goddesses. Less than five percent of people in Taiwan are Christians, or people who follow the teachings of Jesus Christ.

This statue in Taiwan was created to honor the Buddha. The Buddhist religion is based on his teachings.

Language

Most people in Taiwan speak Mandarin Chinese. Mandarin is Taiwan's official language. This language doesn't have an alphabet. Instead, people who write in this

Mandarin Chinese uses characters, such as these, instead of letters.

language use small pictures called characters.

Many people also speak Taiwanese, which is sometimes known as Holo or Minnan. Hakka, which is another Chinese language group, is also spoken in Taiwan.

FACT!

There are more than 50,000 characters in the Chinese language.

Watch Your Tone!

Mandarin Chinese speakers use different tones to mean different things. The meaning of a word can change based on how the speaker says it. A word can have a different meaning if the speaker says it in a high voice or a low voice.

People in Taiwan may speak with different dialects depending on where they're from. A dialect is a form of a language from a certain

Most of the signs for businesses and ads in Taiwan's cities use Chinese characters.

area. Some dialects sound so different that they're hard to understand if you're not from the area where they're spoken.

Taiwan is filled with beautiful art, such as paintings. Calligraphy is also very popular. This art form produces beautiful Chinese characters using a paintbrush.

These painted stones are an example of Taiwanese folk art.

Folk art is popular in Taiwan too. This is a kind of art made by common people that's often connected to community life and is passed down over many years.

FACT!

The National Palace Museum in Taipei holds more than 620,000 works of art and historical objects from China.

Festival Time!

People in Taiwan have many festivals, or special gatherings, during the year. Lunar New Year is an important festival that lasts for around two weeks. The Dragon Boat Festival includes boat races.

Taiwan is filled with beautiful figures **carved** from stone, wood, or bamboo. Temples are often decorated with carved dragons and lions. Dragons and lions are also popular figures in traditional dances.

One of Taiwan's most famous festivals is the Sky Lantern Festival. Beautiful lanterns carrying wishes and prayers are sent into the sky.

Other **performing** arts in Taiwan include opera, which is a way of telling stories through singing, and puppetry, or puppet shows.

Fun and Play

Baseball is one of the most popular sports in Taiwan. People of all ages enjoy playing and watching baseball. There are many teams, and some baseball players from Taiwan end up

Taiwan has played in international baseball games, or games against teams from other countries.

playing in the United States or Japan.

Basketball is also a popular sport in Taiwan. Some people enjoy **martial arts**, golf, and tennis. Soccer (often called football outside of the United

Tai chi is a popular martial art in Taiwan. People exercise with graceful movements.

Away from the City

People who live in crowded cities like to travel to Taiwan's beautiful countryside. Taiwan's national parks are great places for hiking and biking.

States) is also played by many people in Taiwan.

Other people in Taiwan find fun in music. Many people enjoy karaoke, or singing along

Families in Taiwan sometimes hike together in beautiful parks.

to popular music as the words play on a screen. People in Taiwan also like to read books and watch movies and TV shows. They take walks outside, and older people sometimes like to play chess in the park.

People in Taiwan love good food! Rice is served with meat and vegetables. It's eaten in other ways as well. Rice is used to make flour for noodles. Congee is a thick rice porridge

Beef noodle soup is one of Taiwan's national dishes.

that's often eaten for breakfast.

People in Taiwan enjoy beef, chicken, pork, and fish. Food is often served in a spicy or sweet **sauce**. People also enjoy vegetables such as sweet potatoes, radishes, and taro root. Hot pot is

Shaved ice is a tasty dessert served all over Taiwan.

a popular Taiwanese dish that includes meat, eggs, and vegetables that cook in hot soup right on the table.

Tea is the most important drink in Taiwan. People drink tea at home

Bubble tea, which is tea with milk and tiny balls filled with a kind of jelly, came from Taiwan and is now popular around the world.

or out with friends. Teahouses are special places to enjoy tea and meet with friends.

Food on the Go

City streets in Taiwan are filled with food stalls. These stalls sell quick meals such as dumplings, noodles, or fried snacks.

Glossary

carve   To create something by cutting into a surface.

Communist   Relating to a system of government in which the central government owns the things that are needed to make and move goods and there is no private property.

electronic   Operating through the use of many small electrical parts.

ethnic   Of or relating to large groups of people who have the same cultural background.

martial arts   Any of the forms of fighting and self-defense practiced as sports.

perform   To do an activity that often requires training or skill.

protect   To keep safe.

sauce   A usually thick liquid that is poured over or mixed with food.

traditional   Having to do with the ways of doing things in a culture that are passed down over time.

Find Out More

Books

Owings, Lisa. *Taiwan*. Minnetonka, MN: Bellwether Media, 2014.

Somervill, Barbara A. *Taiwan*. New York, NY: Children's Press, 2014.

Website

Britannica Kids: Taiwan

kids.britannica.com/kids/article/Taiwan/345797

This article includes facts about Taiwan's geography, people, and culture.

Video

Kids View: Things to Do in Taipei, Taiwan

www.youtube.com/watch?v=BLjTs-RC8Zg

This video takes viewers on a tour of all the fun things kids can do in Taiwan's capital.

Index

About the Author

Joanne Mattern is the author of more than 250 books for children. She specializes in writing nonfiction and has explored many different places in her writing. Her favorite topics include history, travel, sports, biographies, and animals. Joanne lives in New York State with her family.